PIZZAS

Cooking with Style

Thunder Bay
P·R·E·S·S

Published by
Thunder Bay Press
5880 Oberlin Drive, Suite 400
San Diego, California 92121

Produced by Weldon Russell Pty Ltd
107 Union Street, North Sydney, NSW 2060, Australia

A member of the Weldon International Group of Companies

Copyright © 1994 Weldon Russell Pty Ltd

Publisher: Elaine Russell
Publishing manager: Susan Hurley
Author and home economist: Penny Farrell
Editor: Kayte Nunn
US cooking consultant: Mardee Haidin Regan
Designer: Catherine Martin
Photographer: Rowan Fotheringham
Food stylist: Penny Farrell
Production: Dianne Leddy

Library of Congress Cataloging-in-Publication data

Farrell, Penny, 1965–
    Pizzas / [author, Penny Farrell ; photographer, Rowan Fotheringham].
        p.   cm. — (Cooking with style)
     ISBN 1–57145–003–3 : $13.95
     1. Pizza. I. Title. II. Series.
  TX770.P58F37 1994
  641.8'24—dc20   93–49608
                                                           CIP

Printed by Tien Wah Press, Singapore

A KEVIN WELDON PRODUCTION

Cover: *Goat Cheese, Bell Pepper, Olive and Pesto Pizza*
Back cover: *Japanese Pizza*
Opposite: *Italian Gorgonzola Pizza* (recipe on page 96)

CONTENTS

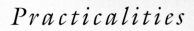

Yeast-risen Pizza Dough

1. Combine 2 teaspoons (⅓ oz/10 g) active dried yeast, 1 teaspoon sugar, ½ teaspoon salt, 1 tablespoon olive oil and ½ cup (4 fl oz/125 ml) water in a bowl. Set aside for 10 minutes, or until frothy.

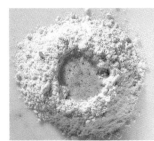

2. Place 1½ cups (6 oz/185 g) all-purpose (plain) flour on a pastry slab or in a large bowl. Make a well in the center and add the yeast mixture.

3. Combine by gradually incorporating the flour into the yeast mixture, adding a little extra water if necessary. (Alternatively, combine the mixture in a food processor.)

4. Transfer to a floured board. Knead until smooth and elastic, about 5 minutes. Place in a large lightly oiled bowl. Cover and place in a warm, draft-free place for 30 minutes or until size doubles.

Yeast-free Pizza Dough

Place 1½ cups (6 oz/185 g) all-purpose (plain) flour*, 1 tablespoon baking powder and ½ teaspoon salt in a bowl. Make a well in the center and add ½ cup (4 fl oz/125 ml) water and 2 tablespoons olive oil. Combine by gradually incorporating the flour into the olive oil and water, adding a little extra water if necessary. (Alternatively, combine the mixture in a food processor.) Transfer the dough to a floured board and knead until smooth and elastic, 5–7 minutes.

Sourdough Pizza Dough

To make the starter: Combine 1 teaspoon active dried yeast and 1 cup (8 fl oz/250 ml) water. Whisk in 1 cup (4 oz/125 g) all-purpose (plain) flour. Cover with plastic wrap and set aside at room temperature for 3 to 24 hours, until frothy. (The longer the souring time, the sourer the dough.) Add ½ teaspoon of salt and 2 cups (8 oz/250 g) all-purpose (plain) flour to the starter. Knead until pliable, about 5 minutes. Set aside in a warm place until it has nearly doubled in size, about 40 minutes. *Makes one 9 inch (22 cm) sourdough base.*

Cornmeal Pizza Dough

Place ½ cup (2½ oz/75 g) yellow cornmeal or polenta, 1 cup (4 oz/125 g) all-purpose (plain) flour*, 2 teaspoons baking powder and ½ teaspoon salt in a bowl. Make a well in the center and add ½ cup (4 fl oz/125 ml) water and 2 tablespoons olive oil. Proceed as for Yeast-free Dough.

Whole-wheat Pizza Dough

Place 1½ cups (7 oz/220 g) whole-wheat flour, 1 tablespoon baking powder and ½ teaspoon salt in a bowl. Make a well in the center and add ½ cup plus 2 tablespoons (5 fl oz/155 g) water and 2 tablespoons olive oil. Proceed as for Yeast-freeDough.

Focaccia Pizza Dough

Combine 2 cups (8 oz/250 g) of all-purpose (plain) flour, with 1 tablespoon active dried yeast, 1¼ cups (10 fl oz/315 ml) water and 1 teaspoon sea salt in a bowl. Beat to mix, cover and set aside in a warm place until it has doubled in size, about 20 minutes.

Place 1½ cups (6 oz/185 g) of flour and 4 tablespoons (2 oz/60 g) butter on a board. Spoon the risen yeast mixture into the center of the flour and gradually combine until all of the flour is incorporated. Knead until smooth and elastic, about 5 minutes.

Divide the dough into 3 equal portions. Press each portion of dough into a 9 inch (22 cm) round. Prick well with a fork. Place each round on an oiled baking sheet. Brush the tops with olive oil. Set the focaccia dough aside in a warm, draft-free place until it has doubled in size, about 40 minutes. Meanwhile, preheat oven to 425°F (220°C /Gas 7).

Bake until golden brown on top, about 25 minutes. Cool on a rack. The extra focaccias can be frozen before or after baking. If preparing the dough in advance, extend the proofing time of the dough by placing it in the refrigerator. *Makes three 9 inch (22 cm) Focaccias*

Semolina Pizza Dough

Place ½ cup (2 oz/60 g) semolina flour, 1 cup (4 oz/125 g) all-purpose (plain) flour*, 2 teaspoons baking powder and ½ teaspoon salt in a bowl. Make a well in the center and add ½ cup (4 fl oz/125 ml) water and 2 tablespoons olive oil. Proceed as for Yeast-free Dough.

Tortilla Pizza Dough

Place ½ cup (6 oz/60 g) all-purpose (plain) flour, 1 cup (4 oz/125 g) tortilla flour (masa harina) or extra-fine cornmeal or millet meal, 2 teaspoons baking powder and ½ teaspoon of salt in a bowl. Make a well in the center and add ⅓ cup (3½ fl oz/100 ml) water and 2 tablespoons olive oil. Proceed as for Yeast-free Dough.

*Self-rising flour can be used instead of the all-purpose flour and baking powder.
Unless otherwise stated, all recipes make one 12 inch (30 cm) base.
All pizza doughs can be made in advance and stored in the refrigerator or freezer until required.

Basic Tomato Sauce

2 large onions
2 cloves garlic
1 tablespoon olive oil
2 lbs (1 kg) ripe tomatoes

1. Peel and finely chop the onions and garlic. Sauté in the olive oil over low heat for approximately 10 minutes, or until they are transparent. Roughly chop the tomatoes and add to the onions.

2. Cook the mixture over a medium heat for 35–40 minutes, or until it begins to thicken. Cool

3. This mixture can be stored in the refrigerator for up to 3 weeks.

Makes 4 cups (2 pints/1 l) Preparation/Cooking Time: 50 minutes

Sun-dried Tomato Sauce
Drain and purée 9½ oz (300 g) sun-dried tomatoes in olive oil. Add the purée, plus 1 tablespoon finely chopped basil leaves to 1 quantity of Basic Tomato Sauce.

Spicy Tomato Sauce
Finely chop 1–2 fresh red or green chilies, or to enough taste, and add to the onions when making 1 quantity of Basic Tomato Sauce.

Pesto

1 large bunch fresh basil, stems removed,
  leaves washed and dried
¼ cup (¾ oz/25 g) pine nuts
½ cup (1¾ oz/50 g) grated Parmesan cheese
2 cloves garlic, peeled
½ cup (4 fl oz/125 ml) olive oil

1. Combine the basil leaves, pine nuts, Parmesan and garlic in a food processor or blender. Blend until smooth.

2. Add the oil very gradually, processing until the mixture is well combined.

3. Store in the refrigerator topped with a film of oil (to prevent discoloration). Any excess pesto may be frozen.

Makes 1½ cups (12 fl oz/375 ml)   Preparation/Cooking Time: 10 minutes

Useful Information for Making Pizza

• A pizza brick or unglazed terracotta tile allows even cooking, ensures a crisp base and hastens the cooking. Pizza bricks also absorb any moisture in the oven and create a drier heat for baking. Be sure to heat the brick as you preheat the oven. If a pizza brick or terracotta tile is unavailable, use a heavy baking sheet.

• To temper a pizza stone or tile for first use, place in a cool oven and gradually heat until the oven temperature reaches 475°F (240°C/Gas 9). Reduce the oven temperature to 450°F (230°C/Gas 8) and the stone will be ready for use. This preliminary tempering is essential to ensure the stone does not crack.

Blue Cheese Pizza

1 large (9½ inch/24 cm) pita or
   lavash bread
½ cup (4 fl oz/125 ml) Basic
   Tomato Sauce (page 10)
3½ oz (100g) blue cheese, such as
   Roquefort, crumbled
¼ cup (1¾ oz/50 g) walnut pieces

Preheat oven to 450°F (230°C/Gas 8).
   Place the pita bread on a baking sheet, spread the tomato sauce over the surface and then top with the crumbled cheese and the walnuts.

   Bake for 15 minutes, or until the pizza is golden on the edges and crisp underneath.

Serves 2–4
Preparation/Cooking Time: 30 minutes

Four Cheese Pizza

1 quantity Yeast-free Pizza
   Dough (page 8)
½ cup (4 fl oz/125 ml) Basic
   Tomato Sauce (page 10)
2 oz (60 g) Romano cheese, grated
2 oz (60 g) provolone cheese, sliced
1 oz (30 g) grated Parmesan
   cheese
2 oz (60 g) grated mozzarella
   cheese

Place a pizza brick, unglazed terracotta tile or baking sheet in the oven. Preheat oven to 450°F (230°C/Gas 8).

On a floured surface, press out the pizza dough using your fingertips into a 9½ inch (24 cm) circle (always pressing from the inside of the dough to the outside).

Place the pizza dough on the heated brick, tile or baking sheet. Spoon on the tomato sauce and arrange the cheeses on top.

Bake for 15 minutes, or until the pizza is golden on the edges and crisp underneath.

Serves 2–4
Preparation/Cooking Time: 30 minutes

Italian Cheese Pizza

1 quantity Cornmeal Pizza
  Dough (page 9)
¼ cup (2 fl oz/60 ml) Sun-dried
  Tomato Sauce (page 10)
3½ oz (100 g) stracchino cheese or
  fresh mozzarella, sliced
2 teaspoons fresh or 1·teaspoon
  dried oregano

Place a pizza brick, unglazed terracotta tile or baking sheet in the oven. Preheat oven to 450°F (230°C/Gas 8).

On a floured surface, press out the pizza dough using your fingertips into an 8 inch (20 cm) circle (always pressing from the inside of the dough to the outside).

Place the pizza dough on the heated brick, tile or baking sheet. Spread the tomato sauce over the surface and then top with the cheese and oregano.

Bake for 15 minutes, or until the pizza is golden on the edges and crisp underneath.

Serves 2–4
Preparation/Cooking Time: 30 minutes

Goat Cheese, Bell Pepper, Olive and Pesto Pizza

1 quantity Yeast-risen Pizza
  Dough (page 8)
1/4 cup (2 fl oz/60 ml) Basic
  Tomato Sauce (page 10)
1/4 cup (2 fl oz/60 ml) Pesto (page
  11)
6 oz (185 g) goat cheese, crumbled
2 red bell peppers (capsicums),
  broiled (grilled), skin removed
  and cut into strips
3 1/2 oz (100 g) black olives, pitted
  and halved lengthwise

Place a pizza brick, unglazed terracotta tile or baking sheet in the oven. Preheat oven to 450°F (230°C/Gas 8).

On a floured surface, press out the pizza dough using your fingertips into a 10 inch (25 cm) circle (always pressing from the inside of the dough to the outside).

Place the pizza dough on the heated brick, tile or baking sheet. Spread with the tomato sauce, pesto and goat cheese.

Bake for 10 minutes, then remove from the oven and top with strips of red bell pepper (capsicum) in a criss-cross pattern. Place one half of an olive in each square between the pepper. Return to the oven for a further 10 minutes, until the base is cooked through.

Serves 2–4
Preparation/Cooking Time: 30 minutes

Chicken Satay Pizza

4 oz (125 g) chicken breast fillet
⅓ cup (2¾ fl oz/80 ml) satay
  (peanut) sauce
1 tablespoon olive oil
1 quantity Cornmeal Pizza
  Dough (page 9)
¼ cup (⅓ oz/10 g) bean sprouts
½ cup (1¾ oz/50 g) grated
  mozzarella cheese

Place a pizza brick, unglazed terracotta tile or baking sheet in the oven. Preheat oven to 450°F (230°C/Gas 8).

Thinly slice the chicken and marinate in 1 tablespoon of the satay sauce and the olive oil. Let marinate for at least 20 minutes.

On a floured surface, press out the pizza dough using your fingertips into a 9 inch (22 cm) circle (always pressing from the inside of the dough to the outside).

Place the pizza dough on the heated brick, tile or baking sheet. Spread with the remaining satay sauce and then top with the chicken, bean sprouts and mozzarella.

Bake for 15 minutes, or until the pizza is golden on the edges and crisp underneath.

Serves 2–4
Preparation/Cooking Time: 50 minutes

Barbecued Chicken Pan Pizza

1 quantity Tortilla Pizza Dough
  (page 9)
½ cup (4 fl oz/125 ml) Basic
  Tomato Sauce (page 10)
8 oz (250 g) barbecued chicken
  meat, shredded
½ cup (3½ oz/100 g) cooked sweet
  corn kernels
¼ cup (30 g/1 oz) grated
  mozzarella cheese
1 tablespoon chopped fresh parsley

Preheat oven to 450°F (230°C/Gas 8).
On a floured surface, press out the pizza dough using your fingertips to fit a 10 inch (25 cm) pizza pan (always pressing from the inside of the dough to the outside).

Spread the tomato sauce over the pizza base. Arrange the chicken, corn and mozzarella over the pizza.

Bake for 15 minutes, or until the pizza is golden on the edges and crisp underneath. Serve sprinkled with the parsley.

Serves 2–4
Preparation/Cooking Time: 30 minutes

Smoked Turkey Pizza

1 quantity Tortilla Pizza Dough
  (page 9)
½ cup (4 fl oz/125 ml) Basic
  Tomato Sauce (page 10)
3½ oz (100 g) smoked turkey,
  sliced
1 small onion, thinly sliced
1 tablespoon capers
1 tablespoon redcurrant or
  cranberry jelly, warmed

Place a pizza brick, unglazed terracotta tile or baking sheet in the oven. Preheat oven to 450°F (230°C/Gas 8).

On a floured surface, press out the pizza dough using your fingertips into a 10 inch (25 cm) circle (always pressing from the inside of the dough to the outside).

Place the pizza dough on the heated brick, tile or baking sheet. Spread the tomato sauce over the base and arrange the smoked turkey, onion and capers over the pizza.

Bake for 15 minutes, or until the pizza is golden on the edges and crisp underneath. Brush with the redcurrant or cranberry jelly and serve.

Serves 2–4
Preparation/Cooking Time: 30 minutes

Smoked Chicken Pizza

1 quantity Whole-wheat Pizza
  Dough (page 9)
½ cup (4 fl oz/125 ml) Basic
  Tomato Sauce (page 10)
8 oz (250 g) smoked chicken, sliced
3½ oz (100 g) goat cheese,
  crumbled

Place a pizza brick, unglazed terracotta tile or baking sheet in the
oven. Preheat oven to 450°F (230°C/Gas 8).

On a floured surface, press out the pizza dough using your
fingertips into an 11 inch (28 cm) circle (always pressing from the
inside of the dough to the outside).

Place the pizza dough on the heated brick, tile or baking sheet.
Spoon the tomato sauce over the base and top with the smoked
chicken. Arrange the goat cheese on top of the pizza.

Bake for 20 minutes, or until the pizza is golden on the edges and
crisp underneath.

Serves 2–4
Preparation/Cooking Time: 35 minutes

Chicken and Fennel Pizza

*1 quantity Sourdough Pizza
   Dough (page 8)*
2 thin slices fennel
8 asparagus tips
*3½ oz (100 g) boneless chicken
   breast*
*½ cup (4 fl oz/125 ml) Basic
   Tomato Sauce (page 10)*
*½ cup (1¾ oz/50 g) grated
   mozzarella cheese*
1 tablespoon olive oil

Place a pizza brick, unglazed terracotta tile or baking sheet in the oven. Preheat oven to 450°F (230°C/Gas 8).

Cut each of the fennel slices in half. Blanch the fennel and asparagus in boiling water for 1 minute. Refresh in cold water. Cut the chicken into thin strips.

On a floured surface, press out the pizza dough, using your fingertips, into an 11 inch (28 cm) circle (always pressing from the inside of the dough to the outside).

Place the pizza dough on the heated brick, tile or baking sheet. Spread the tomato sauce over the surface and then top with the chicken, asparagus, fennel and mozzarella. Brush the top with the oil.

Bake for 15 minutes, or until the pizza is golden on the edges and crisp underneath.

Serves 2–4
Preparation/Cooking Time: 35 minutes

Marinara Pizza

1 quantity Yeast-risen Pizza
  Dough (page 8)
½ cup (4 fl oz/125 ml) Basic
  Tomato Sauce (page 10)
8 oz (250 g) assorted prepared
  seafood: jumbo shrimp (king
  prawns), mussels, calamari
  rings, baby octopus, scallops, etc.
¼ cup (1 oz/30 g) grated
  mozzarella cheese

Place a pizza brick, unglazed terracotta tile or baking sheet in the oven. Preheat oven to 450°F (230°C/Gas 8).

On a floured surface, press out the pizza dough using your fingertips into a 9 inch (22 cm) circle (always pressing from the inside of the dough to the outside).

Place the pizza dough on the heated brick, tile or baking sheet. Spread the tomato sauce over the dough. Arrange the seafood over the top and then sprinkle with the mozzarella.

Bake for 15–20 minutes, or until the pizza is golden on the edges and the seafood is cooked.

Serves 2–4
Preparation/Cooking Time: 30 minutes

Jumbo Shrimp Pizza

1 quantity Yeast-risen Pizza
  Dough (page 8)

¼ cup (2 fl oz/60 ml) Basic
  Tomato Sauce (page 10)

6 cooked jumbo shrimp (scampi),
  shelled and deveined

½ cup (1¾ oz/50 g) grated
  mozzarella cheese

½ teaspoon ground black pepper

1 teaspoon grated lime or lemon
  zest (rind), plus additional zest,
  for garnish

Place a pizza brick, unglazed terracotta tile or baking sheet in the oven. Preheat oven to 450°F (230°C/Gas 8).

On a floured surface, press out the pizza dough using your fingertips into an 8 inch (20 cm) circle (always pressing from the inside of the dough to the outside).

Place the pizza dough on the heated brick, tile or baking sheet. Spread the tomato sauce over the surface and arrange the shrimp (scampi) and mozzarella over the top. Sprinkle with the black pepper and zest (rind).

Bake for 15 minutes, or until the pizza is golden on the edges and crisp underneath. Serve, garnished with the extra zest.

Serves 2–4
Preparation/Cooking Time: 30 minutes

Crab and Chili Pizza

1 quantity Yeast-risen Pizza
  Dough (page 8)
1 cup (8 fl oz/250 ml) Spicy
  Tomato Sauce (page 10)
3½ oz (100 g) cooked crabmeat
2½ oz (75 g) brie or mozzarella
  cheese, cut into finger-length
  strips

Place a pizza brick, unglazed terracotta tile or baking sheet in the oven. Preheat oven to 450°F (230°C/Gas 8).

On a floured surface, press out the pizza dough using your fingertips into a 7 inch (18 cm) circle (always pressing from the inside of the dough to the outside).

Place the pizza dough on the heated brick, tile or baking sheet. Spread the tomato sauce over the surface and arrange the crabmeat and cheese on top.

Bake for 15 minutes, or until the pizza is golden on the edges and crisp underneath.

Serves 2–4
Preparation/Cooking Time: 30 minutes

Bouillabaisse Calzone

2½ oz (75 g) scallops
8 oz (250 g) mussels in the shell
3½ oz (100 g) shelled jumbo
  shrimp (giant prawns)
½ cup (4 fl oz/125 ml) Basic
  Tomato Sauce (page 10)
½ teaspoon saffron threads
2 quantities Semolina Pizza
  Dough (page 9)

Place a pizza brick, unglazed terracotta tile or baking sheet in the oven. Preheat oven to 450°F (230°C/Gas 8).

Clean the scallops and mussels. Remove the beards, drop into boiling water and cook for 2 minutes. Discard any unopened shells. Place in a nonreactive saucepan with the tomato sauce and saffron. Cook over a gentle heat until the seafood is cooked through, about 5 minutes.

On a floured surface, press each pizza dough out to form a 9 inch (22 cm) circle (always pressing from the inside of the dough to the outside).

Divide the filling between the 2 pizzas, placing it on one side of each circle. Fold over each round of dough to form a semicircle and press to seal the edges. Cut 2 air holes in the top of each. Place the calzones on the heated brick, tile or baking sheet.

Bake for 20 minutes, or until the calzones are golden on top and crisp underneath.

Serves 2
Preparation/Cooking Time: 40 minutes

Smoked Trout Pizza

1 quantity Yeast-free Pizza
  Dough (page 8)
1 small smoked trout
3 large green (spring) onions
½ cup (4 fl oz/125 ml) Basic
  Tomato Sauce (page 10)
½ cup (1¾ oz/50 g) grated
  mozzarella cheese

Place a pizza brick, unglazed terracotta tile or baking sheet in the oven. Preheat oven to 450°F (230°C/Gas 8).

On a floured surface, press out the pizza dough, using your fingertips, into a 10 x 6 inch (25 x 15 cm) oval (always pressing from the inside of the dough to the outside).

Remove the head, skin and all bones from the trout. Cut the green (spring) onions in half lengthwise and discard the long, green shoots.

Place the pizza dough on the heated brick, tile or baking sheet. Spread the tomato sauce over the base and arrange the trout and onions on top. Top with the mozzarella.

Bake for 15 minutes, or until the pizza is golden on the edges and crisp underneath.

Serves 2–4
Preparation/Cooking Time: 35 minutes

Caviar Pizza

1 quantity Sourdough Pizza
  Dough (page 8)
1 tablespoon Basic Tomato Sauce
  (page 10)
1 tablespoon crème fraîche
3½ oz (100 g) assorted caviars:
  red caviar, black caviar, salmon
  roe, trout roe, etc.
2 hard-cooked eggs, sliced
1 tablespoon chopped chives

Place a pizza brick, unglazed terracotta tile or baking sheet in the oven. Preheat oven to 450°F (230°C/Gas 8).

On a floured surface, press out the pizza dough using your fingertips into an 8 inch (20 cm) circle (always pressing from the inside of the dough to the outside).

Place the pizza dough on the heated brick, tile or baking sheet. Spread the tomato sauce over the surface.

Bake for 15 minutes, or until the pizza is golden on the edges and crisp underneath.

Remove from the oven and top with the crème fraîche, caviars, egg slices and chives. Return to the oven for a few minutes to quickly heat through. Serve immediately.

Serves 2–4
Preparation/Cooking Time: 35 minutes

Smoked Salmon Pizza

1 quantity Yeast-free Pizza
  Dough (page 8)
½ cup (4 fl oz/125 g) Sun-dried
  Tomato Sauce (page 10)
1 oz (30 g) pickled onions
3½ oz (100 g) smoked salmon
  slices
1 teaspoon capers
1 teaspoon fresh chervil leaves

Place a pizza brick, unglazed terracotta tile or baking sheet in the oven. Preheat oven to 450°F (230°C/Gas 8).

On a floured surface, press out the pizza dough using your fingertips into an 11 inch (28 cm) circle (always pressing from the inside of the dough to the outside).

Place the pizza dough on the heated brick, tile or baking sheet. Spread the tomato sauce over the surface.

Bake for 15 minutes, or until the pizza is golden on the edges and crisp underneath. Allow to cool.

Thinly slice the onions. Arrange them on top of the pizza base with the smoked salmon, capers and chervil. Serve at room temperature.

Serves 2
Preparation/Cooking Time: 1 hour

Thai Shrimp Pizza

1 large (10 x 8-inch/25 x 20-cm)
   pita or lavash bread
1–2 tablespoons Thai sweet chili
   sauce
1–2 teaspoons chopped fresh
   coriander
6½ oz (200 g) cooked and peeled
   large shrimp (king prawns)
½ cup (2½ oz/75 g) chopped
   shallots
1 tablespoon raw, unsalted
   peanuts
a few strips fresh or desiccated
   coconut

Preheat oven to 400°F (200°C/Gas 6).
Place the pita bread on a baking sheet.
   Brush the pita bread with the Thai sweet chili sauce. Sprinkle with the chopped coriander. Top with the shrimp, shallots, peanuts and coconut strips.
   Bake for 3–5 minutes, or until the pizza is heated through. Garnish with a little extra coriander if desired.

Serves 2–4
Preparation/Cooking Time: 15 minutes

Pancetta Pizza

1 quantity Yeast-risen Pizza
  Dough (page 8)
1 cup (8 fl oz/250 ml) Basic
  Tomato Sauce (page 10)
3½ oz (100 g) pepperoni, thinly
  sliced
3½ oz (100 g) pancetta, or
  Italian salami, thinly sliced
½ cup (1¾ oz/50 g) grated
  mozzarella cheese

Place a pizza brick, unglazed terracotta tile or baking sheet in the oven. Preheat oven to 450°F (230°C/Gas 8).

On a floured surface, press out the pizza dough using your fingertips into a 12 inch (30 cm) circle (always pressing from the inside of the dough to the outside).

Place the pizza dough on the heated brick, tile or baking sheet. Spread the tomato sauce over the surface. Arrange the pepperoni, pancetta and the mozzarella over the top.

Bake for 15 minutes, or until the pizza is golden on the edges and crisp underneath.

Serves 2–4
Preparation/Cooking Time: 30 minutes

Japanese-style Pizza

1 quantity Yeast-free Pizza
    Dough (page 8)
8 oz (250 g) pork fillet
2 tablespoons teriyaki glaze*
wasabi paste, to taste
½ cup (4 fl oz/125 ml) Basic
    Tomato Sauce (page 10)
¼ cup (⅓ oz/10 g) bamboo shoots
½ cup (1¾ oz/50 g) grated
    mozzarella cheese
1 tablespoon black sesame seeds

*If teriyaki glaze is unavailable,
    use teriyaki or soy sauce.

Place a pizza brick, unglazed terracotta tile or baking sheet in the oven. Preheat oven to 450°F (230°C/Gas 8).

Trim the pork fillet of any fat and thinly slice. Combine with the teriyaki glaze and set aside to marinate until needed.

On a floured surface, press out the pizza dough, using your fingertips, into a 12 inch (30 cm) circle (always pressing from the inside of the dough to the outside).

Place the pizza dough on the heated stone, tile or baking sheet. Spread a little wasabi over the base, then spoon on the tomato sauce. Top with the pork, bamboo shoots, mozzarella and sesame seeds.

Bake for 15 minutes, or until the pizza is golden on the edges and crisp underneath.

Serves 2–4
Preparation/Cooking Time: 1 hour 30 minutes

Coppa Pizza

1 large (9½ inch/24 cm) pita
    bread
½ cup (4 fl oz/125 ml) Basic
    Tomato Sauce (page 10)
3½ oz (100 g) coppa or cooked
    smoked bacon or ham, thinly
    sliced
2 oz (60 g) pancetta or salami,
    thinly sliced
1¾ oz (50 g) mozzarella cheese,
    thinly sliced
4 cherry tomatoes, halved
1 tablespoon pine nuts
1 teaspoon rosemary leaves
2 teaspoons black olive paste

Preheat oven to 450°F (230°C/Gas 8).
    Place the pita bread on a baking sheet. Spoon the tomato sauce over the pita bread. Arrange the coppa and pancetta on top of the sauce. Top with the mozzarella, tomato halves, pine nuts and rosemary. Dot the olive paste around the pizza.

Bake for 10 minutes or until the cheese is melted.

Serves 2–4
Preparation/Cooking Time: 20 minutes

Roast Garlic and Bacon Pizza

2 whole heads of garlic
4 rashers Canadian (lean) bacon
1 quantity Yeast-free Pizza
    Dough (page 8)
¾ cup (6 fl oz/185 ml) Basic
    Tomato Sauce (page 10)
¾ cup (2½ oz/75 g) grated
    mozzarella cheese

Place a pizza brick, unglazed terracotta tile or baking sheet in the oven. Preheat oven to 450°F (230°C/Gas 8).

Wrap each head of garlic in foil. Bake for 40–45 minutes, or until tender. Cool slightly, then cut each bulb in half and press out the garlic pulp. Discard the husk.

Trim the bacon of all fat and cut into 3–4 inch (8–10 cm) pieces.

On a floured surface, press out the pizza dough, using your fingertips, into a 12 inch (30 cm) circle (always pressing from the inside of the dough to the outside).

Place the pizza dough on your heated brick, tile or baking sheet. Spread the garlic over the surface and then top with tomato sauce. Arrange the bacon strips over the sauce and then sprinkle with the mozzarella.

Bake for 15 minutes, or until the pizza is golden on the edges and crisp underneath.

Serves 2–4
Preparation/Cooking Time: 1 hour 30 minutes

Chili, Pepperoni and Anchovy Pizza

1 quantity Yeast-risen Pizza
  Dough (page 8)
¾ cup (6 fl oz/185 ml) Spicy
  Tomato Sauce (page 10)
5 oz (155 g) pepperoni, thinly
  sliced
6 anchovy fillets
½ cup (1¾ oz/50 g) grated
  mozzarella cheese

Place a pizza brick, unglazed terracotta tile or baking sheet in the oven. Preheat oven to 450°F (230°C/Gas 8).

On a floured surface, press out the pizza dough using your fingertips into an 8 inch (20 cm) circle (always pressing from the inside of the dough to the outside).

Place the pizza dough on the heated brick, tile or baking sheet. Spoon the tomato sauce over the base, then arrange the pepperoni, anchovies and mozzarella on the top.

Bake for 20–25 minutes, or until the pizza is golden and the pepperoni is crisp.

Serves 2–4
Preparation/Cooking Time: 40 minutes

Tuscan Pizza

1 quantity Cornmeal Pizza
 Dough (page 9)
¾ cup (6 oz/185 ml) Sun-dried
 Tomato Sauce (page 10)
6 slices prosciutto
3½ oz (100 g) smoked mozzarella
 cheese, thinly sliced
¼ cup (2 oz/60 g) sliced, roasted
 red bell pepper (capsicum)
1 tablespoon flat-leaf
 (continental) parsley leaves

Place a pizza brick, unglazed terracotta tile or baking sheet in the oven. Preheat oven to 450°F (230°C/Gas 8).

On a floured surface, press out the pizza dough using your fingertips into an 11 inch (28 cm) circle (always pressing from the inside of the dough to the outside).

Place the pizza dough on the heated brick, tile or baking sheet. Spread the tomato sauce over the surface and arrange the prosciutto, mozzarella, bell pepper (capsicum) and parsley over the top.

Bake for 15 minutes or until the pizza is golden on the edges and crisp underneath.

Serves 2–4
Preparation/Cooking Time: 30 minutes

Porcini and Prosciutto Pizza

½ oz (15 g) dried porcini
   mushrooms
1 Focaccia (page 9)
½ cup (4 fl oz/125 ml) Sun-dried
   Tomato Sauce (page 10)
2 slices prosciutto
¼ cup (1 oz/30 g) grated
   mozzarella cheese

Soak the porcini in water or stock to cover for 2 hours. Drain thoroughly and slice any large pieces.

Place a pizza brick, unglazed terracotta tile or baking sheet in the oven. Preheat oven to 450°F (230°C/Gas 8).

Place the focaccia on the heated brick, tile or baking sheet. Spread the tomato sauce over the surface and then top with the mushrooms, prosciutto and mozzarella.

Bake for 15 minutes, or until the pizza is golden on the edges and crisp underneath.

Serves 2–4
Preparation/Cooking Time: 2 hours 30 minutes

Pizza Crusts

1 quantity pizza dough (page 8)
— any dough can be used

Garlic Crusts:
1 tablespoon olive oil
3 cloves garlic, chopped

Chili Crusts:
2 teaspoons chopped chili
1 tablespoon olive oil

Pesto Crusts:
¼ cup (2 fl oz/60 ml) Pesto
(page 11)

Herb Crusts:
1 tablespoon olive oil
2 teaspoons chopped mixed herbs

Place a pizza brick, unglazed terracotta tile or baking sheet in the oven. Preheat oven to 450°F (230°C/Gas 8).

On a floured surface, press out the pizza dough, using your fingertips, into a 10 inch (25 cm) circle (always pressing from the inside of the dough to the outside).

Place the pizza dough on the heated brick, tile or baking sheet. Spread the desired ingredients over the base.

Bake for 15 minutes, or until the pizza is golden on the edges and crisp underneath.

Serve, cut into wedges, with a dip or by themselves. This is a good way to use up any leftover pizza dough.

Serves 6
Preparation/Cooking Time: 30 minutes

Bell Pepper Pizza

1 large red bell pepper (capsicum)

1 large yellow bell pepper (capsicum)

1 large green bell pepper (capsicum)

1 quantity Whole-wheat Pizza Dough (page 9)

2 tablespoons Pesto (page 11)

2 tablespoons grated Parmesan cheese

1 tablespoon pine nuts

Place a pizza brick, unglazed terracotta tile or baking sheet in the oven. Preheat oven to 450°F (230°C/Gas 8).

Grill the bell peppers (capsicums) until their skin just begins to blister. Place in a plastic bag for 10 minutes and then remove the skin, seeds and membranes. Slice into thin strips, keeping the different colors separate.

On a floured surface, press out the pizza dough using your fingertips into a 9 inch (22 cm) circle (always pressing from the inside of the dough to the outside).

Place the pizza dough on the heated brick, tile or baking sheet. Spread the pesto over the surface and then arrange the bell peppers over the top. Sprinkle with the Parmesan and pine nuts.

Bake for 15 minutes, or until the pizza is golden on the edges and crisp underneath.

Serves 2–4
Preparation/Cooking Time: 50 minutes

Eggplant Pizza

1 medium (6½ oz/200 g)
   eggplant (aubergine)
1 tablespoon olive oil
1 Focaccia (page 9)
½ cup (4 fl oz/125 ml) Sun-dried
   Tomato Sauce (page 10)
1 teaspoon fresh basil leaves,
   roughly torn
1¾ oz (50 g) Provolone cheese,
   grated

Place a pizza brick, unglazed terracotta tile or baking sheet in the oven. Preheat oven to 450°F (230°C/Gas 8).

Slice the eggplant (aubergine) into thin rounds. Brush both sides of the eggplant with some of the olive oil and broil (grill) until browned on both sides.

Place the focaccia on the heated brick, tile or baking sheet. Spread the focaccia with the tomato sauce and then top with the eggplant, basil and Provolone.

Bake for 10 minutes, or until heated through.

Serves 4
Preparation/Cooking Time: 25 minutes

Herb Pizza

1 quantity Whole-wheat Pizza
  Dough (page 9)
1 cup (8 fl oz/250 ml) Spicy
  Tomato Sauce (page 10)
1 cup (1 oz/30 g) mixed chopped
  herbs: chervil, rosemary, parsley,
  oregano, marjoram, chives,
  basil, etc.
1 tablespoon poppy seeds
¾ cup (2½ oz/75 g) grated
  mozzarella cheese

Place a pizza brick, unglazed terracotta tile or baking sheet in the oven. Preheat oven to 450°F (230°C/Gas 8).

On a floured surface, press out the pizza dough, using your fingertips, into a 12 inch (30 cm) circle (always pressing from the inside of the dough to the outside).

Place the pizza dough on the heated brick, tile or baking sheet. Spread the tomato sauce over the surface and then top with the herbs, poppy seeds and mozzarella.

Bake for 15 minutes, or until the pizza is golden on the edges and crisp underneath.

Serves 2–4
Preparation/Cooking Time: 30 minutes

Potato Pizza

1 quantity Yeast-free Pizza
   Dough (page 8)
1 lb (500 g) potatoes
2 tablespoons extra virgin olive oil
1 tablespoon rosemary leaves
1 teaspoon cracked black pepper

Place a pizza brick, unglazed terracotta tile or baking sheet in the oven. Preheat oven to 450°F (230°C/Gas 8).

On a floured surface, press out the pizza dough, using your fingertips, into a 12 inch (30 cm) square (always pressing from the inside of the dough to the outside).

Slice the potatoes as thinly as possible.

Place the pizza dough on the heated brick, tile or sheet. Brush the base with a little of the oil, then arrange the potatoes on top. Sprinkle with the rosemary and the pepper and drizzle over any remaining oil.

Bake for 25 minutes, or until the pizza is golden on the edges and crisp underneath.

Serves 4
Preparation/Cooking Time: 40 minutes

Mushroom Pizza

1 quantity Cornmeal Pizza
   Dough (page 9)
2 tablespoons olive oil
8 oz (250 g) assorted mushrooms:
   cèpes, oyster mushrooms, shiitake
   mushrooms, straw mushrooms,
   cultivated mushrooms, etc.,
   sliced if large
¼ cup (2 fl oz/60 ml) Pesto
   (page 11)
½ cup (1¾ oz/50 g) grated
   mozzarella cheese
basil leaves, for garnish

Place a pizza brick, unglazed terracotta tile or baking sheet in the oven. Preheat oven to 450°F (230°C/Gas 8).

On a floured surface, press out the pizza dough using your fingertips into an 11 inch (28 cm) circle (always pressing from the inside of the dough to the outside).

Heat the olive oil over medium heat. Add all of the mushrooms and sauté until almost tender.

Place the pizza dough on the heated brick, tile or baking sheet. Spoon the pesto over the surface and then top with mushrooms. Sprinkle with the mozzarella.

Bake for 15 minutes, or until the pizza is golden on the edges and crisp underneath. Serve sprinkled with the basil leaves.

Serves 4
Preparation/Cooking Time: 35 minutes

Onion Pizza

1 quantity Yeast-free Pizza
  Dough (page 8)
2 tablespoons olive oil
1 yellow onion, thinly sliced
1 white onion, thinly sliced
2 Spanish onions, thinly sliced
3 large green (spring) onions,
  thinly sliced
4 shallots, thinly sliced
¾ cup (6 fl oz/185 ml) Sun-dried
  Tomato Sauce (page 10)

Place a pizza brick, unglazed terracotta tile or baking sheet in the oven. Preheat oven to 450°F (230°C/Gas 8).

On a floured surface, press out the pizza dough, using your fingertips, to form a 12 inch (30 cm) circle (always pressing from the inside of the dough to the outside).

Heat the oil in a frying pan, over medium heat. Add all of the sliced onions and the shallots and sauté until just tender.

Place the pizza dough on the heated brick, tile or baking sheet. Spread the Sun-dried Tomato Sauce over the base and then top with the onions and shallots.

Bake for 15 minutes, or until the pizza is golden on the edges and crisp underneath.

Serves 4
Preparation/Cooking Time: 40 minutes

Diet Pizza

¼ cup (1 oz/30 g) julienned fresh
　baby corn
½ cup (1¾ oz/50 g) julienned
　carrots
¼ cup (1 oz/30 g) julienned snow
　peas (mange tout)
¼ cup (1 oz/30 g) julienned
　zucchini (courgette)
¼ cup (1 oz/30 g) julienned
　yellow bell pepper (capsicum)
1 tablespoon olive oil
8 individual whole-wheat pita
　breads
½ cup (4 fl oz/125 ml) Basic
　Tomato Sauce (page 10)
3½ oz (100 g) low-fat ricotta
　cheese

Preheat oven to 400°F (200°C/Gas 6).
　Heat the olive oil in a small frying pan over medium heat. Add all of the vegetables and sauté until just tender, about 5 minutes.

　Arrange the pita breads on a baking sheet. Top each with some of the tomato sauce, then a little of the cheese. Divide the vegetables among the pita breads and arrange on top.

　Bake for 10–15 minutes, or until heated through.

Serves 4
Preparation/Cooking Time: 25 minutes

Olive Pizza with Pesto

1 quantity Semolina Pizza Dough
  (page 9)
¼ cup (2 fl oz/60 ml) Pesto
  (page 11)
13 oz (410 g) pitted, whole mixed
  olives, such as jumbo black
  olives, Kalamata olives, Spanish
  black olives, Spanish green olives
½ cup (1¾ oz/50 g) grated
  mozzarella cheese

Place a pizza brick, unglazed terracotta tile or baking sheet in the oven. Preheat oven to 450°F (230°C/Gas 7).

On a floured surface, press out the pizza dough, using your fingertips, into a 12 inch (30 cm) circle (always pressing from the inside of the dough to the outside).

Place the pizza dough on the heated brick, tile or baking sheet. Spread with the pesto. Arrange the olives on top and then sprinkle with the mozzarella.

Bake for 15 minutes, or until the pizza is golden on the edges and crisp underneath.

Serves 2–4
Preparation/Cooking Time: 30 minutes

Greek-style Pizza

1 large (9 inch/22 cm) pita bread
1 tablespoon Pesto (page 11)
1 tablespoon black olive paste
3½ oz (100 g) feta cheese, cut into
 ¼ inch (0.5 cm) dice
¾ oz (20 g) pitted Kalamata
 olives

Preheat oven to 400°F (200°C/Gas 6).
 Place the pita bread on a baking sheet. Spread the pesto and olive paste over the bread. Arrange the cheese and olives on top. Bake for 10 minutes, or until crisp.

Serves 1–2
Preparation/Cooking Time: 15 minutes

Swiss Pizza

1 quantity Whole-wheat Pizza Dough (page 9)

½ cup (4 fl oz/125 ml) Basic Tomato Sauce (page 10)

2½ oz (75 g) baby new potatoes, thinly sliced

1 small onion, thinly sliced

1 small dill pickle (gherkin), thinly sliced

1¾ oz (50 g) Swiss or Raclette cheese, thinly sliced

Place a pizza brick, unglazed terracotta tile or baking sheet in the oven. Preheat oven to 450°F (230°C).

On a floured surface, press out the pizza dough using your fingertips into an 11 inch (28 cm) circle (always pressing from the inside of the dough to the outside).

Place the pizza dough on the heated brick, tile or baking sheet. Spread the tomato sauce over the surface and arrange the potato, onion, pickle (gherkin) and cheese on top.

Bake for 15 minutes, or until the pizza is golden on the edges and crisp underneath.

Serves 2–4
Preparation/Cooking Time: 30 minutes

Artichoke and Tomato Pizza

½ cup (4 fl oz/125 ml) Basic
 Tomato Sauce (page 10)
1 tablespoon Pesto (page 11)
1 Focaccia (page 9)
2 plum tomatoes, sliced
2 small balls fresh mozzarella
 cheese (bocconcini), sliced
2 marinated artichoke hearts,
 quartered
1¾ oz (50 g) Parmesan cheese,
 thinly sliced

Place a pizza brick, unglazed terracotta tile or baking sheet in the oven. Preheat oven to 450°F (230°C/Gas 8).

Combine the tomato sauce and pesto.

Place the focaccia on the heated brick, tile or baking sheet. Spread the mixed sauces over the focaccia. Top with the tomatoes, mozzarella slices and artichokes. Arrange the Parmesan over the top.

Bake for 15 minutes, or until the pizza is golden on the edges and crisp underneath.

Serves 2–4
Preparation/Cooking Time: 30 minutes

Mexican Bean Pizza

1 quantity Tortilla Pizza Dough
  (page 9)
2 tablespoons refried beans
1 large ripe tomato, chopped
2 teaspoons chopped fresh chili
½ cup (1¾ oz/50 g) grated
  mozzarella cheese
½ ripe avocado, mashed, for
  serving
1 tablespoon sour cream, for
  serving

Place a pizza brick, unglazed terracotta tile or baking sheet in the oven. Preheat oven to 450°F (230°C/Gas 8).

On a floured surface, press out the pizza dough using your fingertips into an 8 inch (20 cm) circle (always pressing from the inside of the dough to the outside).

Place pizza dough on the heated brick, tile or baking sheet. Spread the refried beans over the base. Combine the chopped tomato with the chili and spread over the beans. Top with the mozzarella.

Bake for 15 minutes, or until the pizza is golden on the edges and crisp underneath.

Serve the pizza with the mashed avocado and sour cream.

Serves 2–4
Preparation/Cooking Time: 30 minutes

Pizza Tatin

Sweet Pizza Dough:

1 cup (4 oz/125 g) all-purpose
   (plain) flour *

½ tablespoon baking powder

⅛ cup (1 oz/30 g) superfine
   (caster) sugar

4 tablespoons (2 oz/60 g) butter

½ egg yolk

about ⅛ cup (1 fl oz/30 ml)
   orange juice

1¾ oz (50 g) butter

½ cup (3½ oz/100 g) superfine
   (caster) sugar

4 (2 lbs/1 kg) Golden Delicious
   apples

cream, for serving

*1 cup (4 oz/125 g) self-rising
   flour can be used instead of the
   all-purpose flour and baking
   powder

Preheat oven to 350°F (180°C/Gas 4).
   Place the flour, baking powder and sugar in a bowl. Rub in the butter. Add the egg yolk and enough of the orange juice to form a manageable dough, the consistency of pastry. (Alternatively, combine the mixture in a food processor).

Wrap the dough in plastic wrap and chill in the refrigerator for 15 minutes.

Melt the butter in a 9 inch (22 cm) ovenproof frying pan. Add the sugar and cook over a medium heat, without stirring, to make a caramel, about 5–8 minutes.

Peel and quarter the apples and add to the pan. Cook gently for 3–4 minutes, tossing until coated with caramel. Arrange over the base of the pan.

Roll out the dough to fit the pan. Gently place the pastry on top of the apples. Bake in the preheated oven for 25 minutes, until golden.

Invert onto a plate and serve hot, with cream.

Serves 4–6
Preparation/Cooking Time: 1 hour 15 minutes

Berry Pizza

2 quantities Sweet Pizza Dough
(page 86)
8 oz (250 g) mascarpone cheese
13 oz (410 g) assorted berries:
strawberries, blueberries,
raspberries, etc.

Preheat oven to 350°F (180°C/Gas 4).
Roll out the dough into a 12 inch (30 cm) circle. Place on a buttered 12 inch (30 cm) pizza pan. Crimp the edges and bake for 20 minutes, or until golden. Cool and transfer to a serving platter.

Spread the mascarpone over the base. Top with the berries and serve.

Serves 8–10
Preparation/Cooking Time: 1 hour 15 minutes

Orange Pizza

Biscuit (Scone) Dough:

1¼ cups (5 oz/155 g) all-purpose
(plain) flour*

1 tablespoon baking powder

⅛ cup (1 oz/30 g) superfine
(caster) sugar

⅓ cup (3 fl oz/90 ml) milk,
approximately

Topping:

zest (rind) of 1 orange, cut into
julienne

½ cup (4 oz/125 g) sugar

½ cup (4 fl oz/125 ml) water

4 oranges

½ cup (4 oz/125 g) cream cheese,
at room temperature

fresh mint sprigs, for decoration

* 1¼ cups (5 oz/155 g) self-rising
flour can be used instead of the
all-purpose flour and baking
powder

Preheat oven to 350°F (180°C/Gas 4).

Biscuit (Scone) Dough: Place the flour, baking powder and sugar in a bowl and mix together. Add enough of the milk to form a manageable dough.

Roll out the biscuit (scone) dough into an 8 inch (20 cm) circle. Place on a buttered pizza pan. Prick the base all over with a fork and crimp or twist the edges of the pastry. Bake for 15 minutes, or until golden. Cool.

Topping: Place the orange zest (rind), sugar and water in a saucepan. Bring to a boil and simmer until the zest is softened, about 3 minutes. Drain and reserve the syrup.

Peel the oranges and remove all of the pith. Cut the oranges into segments, and discard the membranes.

Beat together the cream cheese and reserved syrup until smooth. Spread the cheese over the cooled pizza base. Top with the orange segments and then the candied orange zest. Serve, garnished with mint.

Serves 6–8
Preparation/Cooking Time: 1 hour

Fruit Salad Pizza

2 quantities Biscuit (Scone)
  Dough (page 90)
4 oz (125 g) ricotta cheese
1 tablespoon Cointreau or other
  orange liqueur
1 cup (8 oz/250 g) fresh fruit
  salad: kiwi fruit, banana,
  strawberries, star fruit,
  blueberries, grapes, mandarin
  orange segments, cantaloupe,
  honeydew melon, orange
  segments, passionfruit pulp, etc.

Preheat oven to 350°F (180°C/Gas 4).
  Roll out the biscuit (scone) dough to fit a 12 inch (30 cm) buttered pizza pan. Prick the base all over with a fork and crimp the edges of the base with a fork.
  Bake for 20 minutes, or until cooked and golden. Cool.
  Combine the ricotta and Cointreau. Spread over the pizza base. Top with the fruit salad and serve.

Serves 8–10
Preparation/Cooking Time: 1 hour

Black Forest Pizza

2 quantities Sweet Pizza Dough
(page 86)

8 oz (250 g) semisweet (dark)
chocolate

1¼ cups (10 fl oz/315 ml) heavy
(double) cream

5 oz (155 g) glacéed cherries,
finely chopped

1 oz (30 g) white chocolate

Preheat oven to 350°F (180°C/Gas 4).
Roll out the dough to fit a 12 inch (30 cm) deep pizza pan. Prick the base all over with a fork. Bake for 20 minutes, or until cooked through. Cool.

Melt the semisweet (dark) chocolate over simmering water or in a microwave. Pour half of it on to a marble slab or metal sheet. Cool.

Combine the remaining melted chocolate with the cream. Beat with a wooden spoon until thick. Spread over the pizza base. Arrange the cherries over the chocolate and cream mixture.

Using a sharp knife at a 45° angle, scrape the reserved, cooled chocolate to form thin scrolls or "chocolate bark." Sprinkle the scrolls over the chocolate filling. Grate the white chocolate and sprinkle over the pizza to garnish.

Serves 8–10
Preparation/Cooking Time: 1 hour

Italian Gorgonzola Pizza

1 quantity Semolina Pizza Dough
  (page 9)
¾ cup (6 fl oz/185 ml) Sun-dried
  Tomato Sauce (page 10)
¼ cup (¼ oz/7.5 g) chopped chives
5 oz (155 g) Gorgonzola cheese,
  crumbled

This recipe is pictured on page 3.

Place a pizza brick, unglazed terracotta tile or baking sheet in the oven. Preheat oven to 450°F (230°C/Gas 8).

On a floured surface, press out the pizza dough using your fingertips into a 12 inch (30 cm) circle (always pressing from the inside of the dough to the outside).

Place the pizza dough on the heated brick, tile or baking sheet. Spread the base with the tomato sauce and sprinkle with the chives. Sprinkle the cheese over the pizza.

Bake for 15 minutes, or until the pizza is golden on the edges and crisp underneath.

Serves 2–4
Preparation/Cooking Time: 30 minutes